FACING YOUR FEAR OF SPEAKING UP

BY MARI SCHUH

PEBBLE
a capstone imprint

Published by Pebble Emerge, an imprint of Capstone
1710 Roe Crest Drive, North Mankato, Minnesota 56003
capstonepub.com

Library of Congress Cataloging-in-Publication Data is available on the Library of Congress website.
ISBN: 9780756570873 (hardcover)
ISBN: 9780756571436 (paperback)
ISBN: 9780756570972 (ebook PDF)

Summary: Describes the fear of speaking up and simple ways readers can gain confidence to stand up for themselves.

Editorial Credits
Editor: Erika L. Shores; Designer: Dina Her; Media Researcher: Jo Miller; Production Specialist: Tori Abraham

Image Credits
Getty Images: kali9, 12, 16, SDI Productions, 19, SolStock, 7; Shutterstock: Africa Studio, 21, Domira (background), cover and throughout, greenland, 13, Kapitosh (cloud), cover and throughout, KatsiarynaKa2, 11, Marish (brave girl), cover and throughout, Monkey Business Images, 6, 17, Pressmaster, 9, Rawpixel.com, 18, Rido, 10, Sengchoy Int, Cover, SeventyFour, 4, stockfour, 5, YAKOBCHUK VIACHESLAV, 15

All internet sites appearing in back matter were available and accurate when this book was sent to press.

Printed and bound in China. PO5130

TABLE OF CONTENTS

Words in **bold** are in the glossary.

FEARS AND WORRIES

Are you ever afraid to speak up? Maybe you need help with schoolwork. Maybe you want to tell a friend that you don't want to play. But you are scared to speak up, so you say nothing.

Many people are scared to speak up. It is normal to feel that way. Facing your fears can help you tell people what you think and feel.

Why are people scared to speak up? It can make them **nervous**. They might worry about what people will say. They could be scared that people will laugh at them.

People might try to ignore things.

They might try to forget about it.

But that does not make it go away.

It does not make things better.

You might worry you will lose friends if you speak up. Everyone thinks and feels differently. It is OK that you and your friends like different things. Good friends know that people are not all the same. They know that people do not always agree. Good friends will understand!

SPEAKING UP

People can speak up about things that are wrong. They can help make things right. A new teacher said Kianna's name the wrong way. Todd is being **bullied**.

People can ask for things they need and want. Diego's cat is sick. He asks his dad for a hug. Jenna asks the school nurse for an ice pack. Ty asks a teacher for help with a math problem.

When some people try to speak up, they talk quietly. They are shy. They do not tell people how they really feel. They do not stand up for themselves. Why? They might be very worried about what other people will think.

Some people speak up in a loud, mean way. They are **rude** and pushy. They might yell. They are only thinking about themselves. They are not thinking about other people.

BELIEVING IN YOURSELF

What is the best way to speak up?
Think of yourself and also think of
other people. How? Talk in a firm,
strong way that is also **polite** and calm.
Be **honest** about what you think and
feel. Be **confident** and brave.

Talking like this shows you **respect**
yourself. It shows you respect others too.
It shows that everyone matters.

When you are ready, you can **practice** speaking up. It can lessen your fears. Join a team or club. Tell your new friends what you like. Talk with adults you trust. Share your feelings.

Be patient as you practice. Speaking up will get easier. Start with small things. Tell friends your favorite kind of pizza. Later, practice saying no. Don't want to go to a friend's sleepover? Say no politely.

Believing in yourself helps you face your fears. You might still be afraid to speak up. But you can have confidence in yourself. You are brave. You can handle your fears.

PRACTICE YOUR BODY LANGUAGE

When you talk, your words are not the only thing that matter. How you move your body matters too. Your body tells people how you are feeling. Be confident with your body. It can help you face your fear of speaking up.

What You Need

- large mirror
- chair
- friend or adult

What You Do

1. Sit in a chair. Look in a mirror. Or have a friend tell you how you look. Are you slouching? Sit up straight and look up. Sitting up straight shows confidence.

2. Now stand up. Look in the mirror. Be sure to put your shoulders back. Walk across the room. Do not slouch. Walk tall with your head up.

3. Talk with your friend. Pretend your friend said something hurtful. Tell them how you feel. Practice talking in a polite way. Look them in the eyes when you talk. If that is too hard, try to look at their nose instead.

Be mindful of how you feel. How does your body feel? Did you feel confident in speaking up?

GLOSSARY

bully (BUL-ee)—to be mean, scare, or pick on someone

confident (KON-fi-duhnt)—sure of yourself

honest (ON-ist)—to be truthful

nervous (NUR-vuhs)—being worried or anxious

polite (puh-LITE)—being kind, respectful, and having good manners

practice (PRAK-tiss)—to keep working to get better at a skill

respect (ri-SPEKT)—to believe in the quality and worth of others and yourself

rude (ROOD)—unkind and not thinking of other people

READ MORE

Kaufman, Gershen. *Stick Up for Yourself!: Every Kid's Guide to Personal Power and Positive Self-Esteem.* Minneapolis: Free Spirit Publishing, 2019.

Lindeen, Mary. *Feeling Afraid.* Chicago: Norwood House Press, 2022.

McAneney, Caitie. *Sometimes We Feel Afraid.* New York: Cavendish Square Publishing, 2022.

INTERNET SITES

KidsHealth: Assertiveness
kidshealth.org/en/teens/assertive.html

KidsHealth: Talking About Your Feelings
kidshealth.org/en/kids/talk-feelings.html

Stop Bullying: What Kids Can Do
stopbullying.gov/resources/kids

INDEX

ABOUT THE AUTHOR

Mari Schuh's love of reading began with cereal boxes at the kitchen table. Today she is the author of hundreds of nonfiction books for beginning readers. Mari lives in the Midwest with her husband and their sassy house rabbit. Learn more about her at marischuh.com.